105090981

MARISSA MAYER

BY SARA GREEN

BELLWETHER MEDIA • MINNEAPOLIS, MN

Jump into the cockpit and take flight with Pilot books. Your journey will take you on high-energy adventures as you learn about all that is wild, weird, fascinating, and fun!

This edition first published in 2015 by Bellwether Media, Inc.

No part of this publication may be reproduced in whole or in part without written permission of the publisher. For information regarding permission, write to Bellwether Media, Inc., Attention: Permissions Department, 5357 Penn Avenue South, Minneapolis, MN 55419.

Library of Congress Cataloging-in-Publication Data

Green, Sara, 1964
  Marissa Mayer / by Sara Green.
      pages. cm. – (Pilot: Tech Icons)
  Summary: "Engaging images accompany information about Marissa Mayer. The combination of high-interest subject matter and narrative text is intended for students in grades 3 through 7"– Provided by publisher
  Audience: Age 7-12.
  Includes bibliographical references and index.
  ISBN 978-1-60014-991-7 (hardcover : alk. paper)
  1. Mayer, Marissa, 1975–Juvenile literature. 2. Yahoo! Inc.–Juvenile literature. 3. Internet industry–United States–Juvenile literature. 4. Businesswomen–United States–Biography–Juvenile literature. I. Title.
  HD9696.8.U62M494 2014
  338.7'6102504092–dc23
  [B]
                                2014014026

Printed in the United States of America, North Mankato, MN.

TABLE OF CONTENTS

News

Finance

CHAPTER 1

WHO IS MARISSA MAYER?

Only a handful of women are in charge of technology companies. Marissa Mayer is one of them. She is the president and CEO of an Internet company called Yahoo. Marissa is a powerful leader in an industry where men outnumber women. Women all over the world see her as a role model. Marissa has big plans for Yahoo. She wants it be an inspiring and entertaining part of people's daily lives. If she has her way, Yahoo will soon be the most popular Internet web portal on Earth.

Marissa is well known in the business world. In 2008, *Fortune* magazine listed her as one of most powerful women in business. At age 33, she was the youngest person on the list! She has been on the list each year following. Marissa's business skills have also earned her a lot of money. Today, she is worth more than $300 million.

ICON BIO

Name: Marissa Ann Mayer

Birthday: May 30, 1975

Hometown: Wausau, Wisconsin

Marital status: Married to Zachary Bogue since 2009

Children: One boy

Hobbies/ Interests: Art, fashion, running, cooking, traveling

Marissa was born in Wausau, Wisconsin, on May 30, 1975. Her parents are Margaret, an art teacher, and Michael, an engineer. She has a younger brother named Mason. Marissa's childhood was loaded with activities. She enjoyed ice skating, swimming, and playing the piano. Marissa also loved ballet. In middle school, she practiced 35 hours a week. In high school, Marissa was a star on the debate team and president of the Spanish club. She was also captain of the pom-pom squad.

From a young age, Marissa loved to learn. She earned top grades in all of her classes. Her favorites were math and science. She was the **valedictorian** of her graduating class of 1993. After graduating, Marissa earned a special honor. The Governor of Wisconsin selected her to attend the National Youth Science Camp in West Virginia. She was one of two students from her state. There, she joined students from around the country to study science and leadership skills.

TEACHER APPRECIATION

In 2010, Marissa entered the Wausau School District's Alumni Hall of Fame. In her speech, she was near tears as she thanked her favorite teachers for their guidance.

CHAPTER 2

STANFORD YEARS

In 1993, Marissa entered Stanford University in Palo Alto, California. Her **major** was pre-medicine. She wanted to become a brain surgeon for children. However, Marissa grew bored with her coursework. She decided to try something different. During her freshman year, Marissa took a class in computer science. Programming came easily to her, and she earned a high grade. Marissa continued to take computer science classes. Her talent impressed the professors. With their encouragement, Marissa changed her major to **symbolic systems**.

Marissa focused her studies on **artificial intelligence**. She enjoyed figuring out how to teach computers to think like people. During this time, Marissa discovered that she also loved to teach people. She became a teaching assistant in computer classes. Marissa was a natural teacher who earned high praise from her students. In 1997, Marissa received her bachelor's degree in symbolic systems. She stayed at Stanford for two more years to pursue a master's degree.

CHAPTER 3
A LEADER AT GOOGLE

In 1999, Marissa received her master's degree in computer science. Right away, she had 14 job offers! One came from a **startup** company called Google. After careful thought, she decided to accept the job at Google. The company was young and full of smart, ambitious people. Marissa would fit right in. She knew she could help the company grow.

Marissa started at Google a week after graduating from Stanford. She was Google's twentieth employee and its first female engineer. She was immediately recognized as an outstanding leader and programmer. In 2005, Marissa became a vice president. Thousands of Google employees reported to her. With her critical eye, Marissa helped develop and design more than 100 Google features. These included the homepage, email, news, and map services. Millions of people around the world use these products. Marissa also found time to teach. She taught a computer science course at Stanford and a management class at Google.

CHAPTER 4

TAKING CHARGE OF YAHOO

After 13 years at Google, Marissa was ready for a change. In 2012, she became the CEO of Yahoo. Marissa knew that Yahoo had problems. Once an **innovative** web site, Yahoo had lost much of its popularity. It had not kept pace with Google and other technology companies. It was losing money, and employee **morale** was low. Marissa was ready for these challenges. She was determined to make Yahoo a successful company again.

Every day, people use mobile phones and tablets to check email, weather, and the news. People also use them for **apps**, games, and videos. Marissa decided to shift Yahoo's focus to **mobile services** like these. She started buying startup companies that specialized in mobile services and products. She then hired their employees to build apps and develop other technologies. At the beginning of 2014, Yahoo owned 37 startups. Marissa's efforts have paid off. More than 800 million people use Yahoo's services every month!

"I always did something
I was a little not ready
to do. I think that's
how you grow."
— Marissa Mayer

Marissa also focused on boosting morale at Yahoo. To improve communication and teamwork, Marissa had walls in the office removed. She decided that employees had to work in the office instead of from home to keep them focused. Marissa started a weekly meeting where people could discuss problems and solutions. She also wanted her employees to feel pride in their work. Marissa encouraged them to have big goals and new ideas. She invited people to stop by her office to discuss plans for Yahoo's future.

Marissa showed support for her employees in other ways. New parents started to receive special benefits. Both moms and dads got $500 and 8 weeks to spend with a new baby. Everyone got a new smartphone. Marissa also made cafeteria food free. Not everyone approved of Marissa's changes. Some left Yahoo for jobs at other companies. However, most employees like Marissa's new policies. Yahoo's future looks bright!

PLEASE CONSIDER ME

In 2013, Yahoo received more than 340,000 job applications. This was double the number received in 2012.

CHAPTER 5

FAMILY LIFE

Marissa is not only a powerful CEO. She is also a wife and mother. In 2007, a friend from Google introduced Marissa to Zachary Bogue. He was a successful banker and lawyer. The two began dating and soon fell in love. On December 12, 2009, they got married in San Francisco. Marissa and Zach work long hours at their jobs. However, they spend time together every chance they get. They especially enjoy running, cooking, and traveling together.

Two months after starting her job at Yahoo, Marissa gave birth to a son named Macallister. She welcomed the challenge of being a mom and a CEO. After a short **maternity leave**, she made space for a nursery next to her office. With this arrangement, she can succeed in both roles.

FASHIONISTA
Marissa loves fashion. One of her favorite designers is Oscar de la Renta.

CHAPTER 6

HELPING OTHERS SUCCEED

Marissa's days are full. However, she still finds time to help other organizations. She is on the **board of directors** of the San Francisco Ballet, the San Francisco Museum of Modern Art, and the New York City Ballet. As a board member, Marissa attends many meetings. She offers advice and helps make important decisions about how the organizations operate. She also helps her community in other ways. For many years, Marissa worked with students at the East Palo Alto Charter School in California. She helped the students learn skills to get into college.

A PASSION FOR ART

Marissa is a devoted art collector. She owns pieces created by some of the most famous artists in the world.

As a technology leader, Marissa is a role model for people all over the world. She cares about her employees. But she is also committed to making products users love. Marissa plans to make Yahoo even more personal. Exciting new apps will target each user's interests. Mobile magazines will update users on news and entertainment. With Marissa in command, Yahoo is coming back stronger than ever!

RESUME

Education

1997-1999: Stanford University, M.S. Computer Science (Palo Alto, California)

1993-1997: Stanford University, B.S. Symbolic Systems (Palo Alto, California)

1989-1993: Wausau West High School (Wausau, Wisconsin)

Work Experience

July 2012-present: President and CEO, Yahoo

2005-2012: Vice President, Google

2003-2005: Director, Consumer Web Services, Google

2001-2003: Product Manager, Google

1999-2001: Software Engineer, Google

Community Service/Philanthropy

- Board member of the San Francisco Museum of Modern Art, San Francisco Ballet, and New York City Ballet

2013: Participated in an online auction to raise money for the Aspire East Palo Alto Charter School, East Palo Alto, California

2012: Donated to Golden Gate Park, San Francisco, California

LIFE TIMELINE

May 30, 1975:
Born in Wausau, Wisconsin

June 23, 1999:
Joins Google as the company's twentieth employee and first female engineer

Google™

May 1993:
Graduates from Wausau West High School, Wausau, Wisconsin

June 1997:
Graduates with honors from Stanford University with a B.S. in Symbolic Systems

June 1999:
Graduates from Stanford University with an M.S. in Computer Science

2008:
Receives an honorary doctorate from the Illinois Institute of Technology

September 30, 2012:
Gives birth to son Macallister

December 12, 2009:
Marries Zachary Bogue

YAHOO!

July 16, 2012:
Becomes President and CEO of Yahoo

2013:
Ranked number 32 in the *Forbes* magazine's list of the world's most powerful women

GLOSSARY

apps—small, specialized programs downloaded onto smartphones and other mobile devices

artificial intelligence—an area of computer science that deals with giving machines the ability to seem like they have human intelligence

board of directors—a group of people who oversee the activities of a company or organization

CEO—Chief Executive Officer; the CEO is the highest-ranking person in a company.

industry—a group of businesses that provide a particular product or service

innovative—introducing new ideas and methods

major—a course of study for a specific degree

maternity leave—time off given to a mother to take care of a newborn

mobile services—communication services to users of smartphones and tablet personal computers

morale—the confidence and enthusiasm of a person or group

startup—a new business

symbolic systems—a course of study that involves the study of language, knowledge, human thought, and computer science

valedictorian—the top student in a graduating class

web portal—a web site that provides a wide variety of services such as email, games, social networks, and information

TO LEARN MORE

AT THE LIBRARY

Harris, Michael C. *Artificial Intelligence*. New York, N.Y.: Marshall Cavendish Benchmark, 2011.

Sutherland, Adam. *The Story of Google*. New York, N.Y.: Rosen Central, 2012.

Tougas, Shelley. *Girls Rule! Amazing Tales of Female Leaders*. North Mankato, Minn.: Capstone Press, 2014.

ON THE WEB

Learning more about Marissa Mayer is as easy as 1, 2, 3.

1. Go to www.factsurfer.com.

2. Enter "Marissa Mayer" into the search box.

3. Click the "Surf" button and you will see a list of related web sites.

With factsurfer.com, finding more information is just a click away.

INDEX